pickle juice

hardie grant books

A revolutionary approach to making
better-tasting cocktails and drinks

pickle juice

By Florence Cherruault

Features: Shrubs, Kimchi, Bloody Marys, Chasers and more

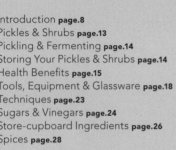

6

Pickle juice & Shrubs

Contents

Introduction

About me, the pickle house

&

how I got started

Pickling and concocting has become somewhat the norm in my day-to-day life. There's always an array of things pickling in jars on the kitchen counter, and bowls of different fruits and herbs macerating in our conservatory at the back of the house to keep them cool. Friends often joke it's like they're in a school science lab as I emerge with different concoctions for them to try.

This book brings together my experiments in the world of pickling with the knowledge of bartenders and mixologists to create a collection of recipes for pickle juices, drinking vinegars and cocktails – both alcoholic and non-alcoholic.

Florence
Cherruault

I've always loved the sharp, briny taste of pickles. There's something about the vinegary tang that makes eating them a bit of a challenge, but it's oh so worth it. My absolute favourites are the little cornichons you get in French supermarkets, but a packet of pickled onion Monster Munch is always my go-to for that 'morning after the night before' feeling.

It was while on holiday in New York that I first tried a Pickleback. The idea of throwing back a shot of whisky followed by a shot of pickle juice seemed like a strange one, but my boyfriend insisted I give it a go… I was hooked.

Once back in London, I started experimenting with different recipes, aiming to create a pickle juice perfect for drinking; one that would go way beyond the leftover brine found at the bottom of a jar of pickles.

After many months developing the recipe, I came up with a blend of sliced cucumbers and spices that I brewed for around 12 weeks to create a sweet-and-savoury flavour that packs a real punch.

In 2014, I decided to launch The Pickle House and sell my Original Pickle Juice. The first batch made 10 bottles, so I decided to go to 10 different bars around London to see what they thought. I started off at Oslo, which had just opened in Hackney Central. The bar manager ordered 40 bottles for that weekend. I was so excited that it took me a second to realise there was no way I could fulfill his order in time. Thankfully, he was happy to wait.

As with any strong-flavoured product, like Marmite, for example, some people loved the pickle juice and some weren't so keen, but once a few bartenders were on board with it, they started coming up with some great pickle-based cocktails.

One drink they all loved was the Bloody Mary, which led me to launch my Bloody Mary Mix: a blend of tomato juice, fresh horseradish, spices and pickle juice.

I never would have thought that when I 'grew up' I'd be making pickle juice, but here I am!

Pickles

&

Pickling and shrub-making are similar in that both methods were used to preserve surplus fruit and vegetables prior to the invention of refrigerators. Pickling has been around for a long time and has been said to date way back to 2,400 BC, whereas shrubs are said to have originated in 17th-century England.

The main difference between the two is that pickles are usually savoury and tend to use vegetables pickled in a salty, vinegary brine. Shrubs are the sweeter version, using predominantly fruits (and some vegetables) macerated in sugar to create a sweet, vinegary syrup.

It was a couple of months after launching my Original Pickle Juice that I discovered all the health benefits. Apple cider vinegar with the 'mother' has been used for centuries as a natural health remedy to fight coughs and colds. The 'mother' looks like a cloudy substance that sits at the bottom of the bottle and, much like a SCOBY (symbiotic culture of bacteria and yeast)

in kombucha, it's full of good bacteria along with acetic acid and natural protein, which is great for your health. Drinking vinegar, be it in pickle juice or a shrub, can help improve digestion, lower blood-sugar levels, support your immune system and, seriously, the list goes on! It's also meant to be great for your skin and nails.

The pickle juice recipes in this book include apple cider vinegar and salt, packing them full of electrolytes ideal for rehydrating your body, whether you're suffering from a hangover or post-workout cramps. Some of the recipes call for turmeric which, like apple cider vinegar, has a huge list of health and medicinal benefits thanks to its anti-inflammatory and antioxidant properties.

Although I first discovered the idea of drinking pickle juice in the form of a Pickleback in New York in 2013, I know it's been around a lot longer. Many have claimed they discovered the Pickleback, but, having spoken to a lot of Pickleback connoisseurs,

most seem to agree that it was a guy called Reggie Cunningham from the Bushwick Country Club in New York. That said, I remember taking a bottle of pickle juice to a friend's house a few years ago and her mum was so excited. She began telling me how, growing up in Poland, they would have shots of vodka then eat pickles and sip on the leftover brine from the bowl.

It's hard to pinpoint exactly when pickle juice and shrubs started being used in cocktails, but the idea of drinking vinegar to aid weight loss has been around for decades. It is believed to help suppress your appetite and make you feel fuller for longer.

I can't back that with any personal proof, but I can say that adding pickle juice and shrubs to cocktails is delicious. Each add a rich, umami flavour that is different to any other drink you'll find on a menu; the vinegar adds a depth of flavour that works so well in both alcoholic and non-alcoholic cocktails.

Shrubs

Pickling & Fermenting

What's the difference between picking and fermenting? The age-old question, I get asked this constantly! Pickling and fermenting are similar in the idea that both methods are used to naturally preserve foods and the final results have a slightly sharp, tangy flavour. The main difference is that the sharp, tangy flavour found in pickling comes from using vinegar or another acidic liquid. Whereas with fermenting, the flavour comes from a chemical reaction between the sugars found in food and naturally present bacteria. The bit that makes it slightly confusing is that some pickles can be fermented and some fermented foods can be pickled.

To compare the two in a bit more detail; when it comes to pickling, although you're using vinegar, which is a product of fermentation, the pickling juice is brought to the boil to allow the salt and sugar to dissolve, which in effect ends up killing and stopping the growth of any microorganisms. Therefore, pickling doesn't have the same probiotic qualities that fermented foods have.

When it comes to fermentation, I spoke to the good guys down at Jarr Kombucha, in London, to find out what their definition of fermenting is. They said in its simplest form, it's the breakdown of a substance by bacteria, yeast or other living microorganisms. Basically, when fruits or vegetables are left in an airtight container their natural bacteria begin to break down the sugars found in these foods and converts them into an acid.

This process is called lacto-fermentation and is what gives fermented food its sharp, tangy flavour, whilst also creating probiotics, which are really good for your digestion. Examples of fermented foods and drinks are kombucha, kimchi (see page 38 for my recipe), yoghurt, sauerkraut and miso.

Storing Your Pickles & Shrubs

Pickles & Pickle Juice
Pickles can last for absolutely ages as long as your jars have been properly sterilised (see page 23). Unopened, you can store your pickles for a year, but, once opened, I'd recommend storing them in the refrigerator and eating them within 1 month. The juice can be kept up for up to 4 months.

Shrubs
Once your shrubs are ready to go, make sure you decant them into sterilised bottles or jars (see page 23), then store in the refrigerator. They should keep for up to 2 months, but if they start to go slimy, fizzy and ferment, throw them away and make a new batch.

Health Benefits

Pickle Juice

I know the idea of drinking pickle juice may not be the most appealing. Actually, I know for a fact that it's not after the amount of very confused, even slightly disgusted faces I see when they first set their eyes on a bottle of pickle juice. But trust me, it's worth a try and if you're not so keen the first time, try it again! Here are some of the main reasons why drinking pickle juice is good for you:

1. Soothes Muscle Cramps

Many athletes drink pickle juice after working out to help ease muscle cramps. I've seen photos of American footballers (soccer players) sitting on the sidelines downing huge jars filled with pickle juice. The high concentration of sodium and vinegar helps relieve muscle aches quickly.

2. Keeps You Hydrated

Thanks to the electrolytes found in pickle juice, it helps your body recover and rehydrate quickly. If you're doing a high intensity work out and sweating a lot then pickle juice could be a better option then water. It's also got much less sugar than all the energy drinks out there.

3. Boosts Your Immune System

Pickle juice contains vitamins C and E, which are two of the primary antioxidants to help boost your immune system.

4. Weight Loss

Drinking a small amount of vinegar everyday can be beneficial for weight loss, and with vinegar being one of the main ingredients in pickle juice, it's worth a try.

Shrubs/Drinking Vinegars

Shrubs have many of the same health benefits as pickle juice, thanks to vinegar being one of the main ingredients. However, when it comes to making shrubs, the vinegar is not heated, which means if you choose an apple cider vinegar that contains the mother it'll keep all its good bacteria. One thing I'd say is if you've got more of a sweet tooth, shrubs are an easier way of getting into vinegar drinking than drinking pickle juice, as they're much sweeter.

Fermented Food & Drink

Rich in probiotic bacteria, fermented foods and drinks are really good for your gut, digestion and immune system. It has been said that if your gut is happy then your mind is happy, because gut is lined with neurons that can change how you feel. All in all, making pickles, shrubs and anything fermented are a quick, cheap and convenient way to avoid waste by being able to preserve any extra fruit and veg you may have lying around. Many bars and restaurants are using their leftover pickle juice for cocktails and making their own drinking vinegars. They really add a great savoury note to cocktails; be it alcoholic or non-alcoholic.

Tools, Equipment

Here are some of the basic tools, equipment and glassware you'll need to help make the recipes in this book. Don't worry if you don't have the exact spoon bartenders use or a proper drinks muddler, you can always use a normal spoon or the end of a wooden rolling pin.

Bar Spoon
Long-handled spoon that allows you to reach the bottom of the tallest glass. The spoon itself is a good measuring tool, as it's about the same as a teaspoon: 5 ml (¼ fl oz).

Blender
A good-quality blender is very useful when it comes to blending ice and ingredients. When making shrubs, I sometimes find you get a richer colour and flavour when the fruit or vegetables are blended before they're macerated with the sugar.

Citrus Press
A quick and easy way to extract the juice from citrus fruits. I like to press quite a few lemons at one time then pour the juice into a bottle and store it in the refrigerator for up to a week.

Cocktail Stick
Highly necessary when it comes to creating some good looking cocktails with great garnishes. I like to use those wooden kebab skewers, I find the toothpick ones slightly too small. With the larger ones you can always cut them down to the right size. There are also some really nice reusable metal ones out there if you want something a little more fancy.

Cutting Board
A wooden cutting board is ideal for cutting up your ingredients, then, when serving cocktails, a smaller board is always handy for peeling or slicing garnishes.

Funnel
When your shrubs and pickle juices are ready, a funnel is a hassle-free way of transferring them to glass bottles.

Glass Bottles/Jugs
Keep your pickle juices and shrubs in glass bottles; it makes them easier to refrigerate and serve.

Hawthorne Strainer
Some cocktail shakers have a strainer built into the top. If not, grab yourself a hawthorne strainer to keep the ice out of your mixed drink.

Juicer
A juicer is a great addition when it comes to making cocktails and, again, I'd recommend getting a good-quality one as they last a lot longer. If you don't have a juicer, you could blend the fruit or vegetables in a blender then strain, but this won't achieve exactly the same consistency.

Kilner Jars
Many of the pickle juice and shrub recipes in this book need to be left for a few hours or days in an airtight container. Glass jars are great for this as they are easy to sterilise (see page 23) and can be reused again and again.

Knives
Always keep your knives sharp. A small one is good for slicing garnishes, but you'll need a bigger one when it comes to cutting up the cabbage for the Kimchi (see page 38) or the watermelon for the Watermelon Shrub (see page 53).

Measuring Spoons
These usually come in a set of 5 different measuring spoons: 1 tablespoon, ½ tablespoon, 1 teaspoon, ½ teaspoon and ¼ teaspoon. My mum gave me an extra set she had and they just make everything so much easier especially when all your tablespoons seem to be different sizes.

Muddler
A bartender's tool a bit like a pestle with a rounded end that is used to muddle fruit, herbs or spices in the bottom of a glass to release their flavour.

Muslin (cheesecloth)
Finely-woven food-grade cotton, ideal for straining the finely chopped fruit or vegetables from the sugar syrup when making shrubs.

& Glassware

Peeler
I like to use a hand-held Y-shape peeler as it gives you more control. Good for making cocktail garnishes like cucumber ribbons or citrus twists and peels.

Shaker
Try finding a cocktail shaker that comes with a strainer, as it makes everything a lot easier. Shakers are used for mixing cocktails by putting all the ingredients in the shaker and shaking for about 10 seconds. When ice is added to the shaker, it cools the drink quickly, allowing you to serve the drink without ice and, therefore, not dilute it.

Sieve
Ideal for separating larger chopped fruit or vegetables from the sugar syrup when making shrubs, or the pickles from the pickle juice.

Spirit Measure
Every home should have a spirit measure even for non-alcoholic cocktails. A dual measure is good, as it has a 25 ml (¾ fl oz) measure on one side and a 50 ml (1¾ fl oz) measure on the other.

Zester
For removing the zest of citrus fruits. Check out the recipe for Chilli Lime Salt, used for rimming the glass of drinks like the Michelada (see page 75).

Champagne Flute
A tall elongated stemmed glass for drinking Champagne, prosecco and sparkling wines. Generally holds around 180–300 ml (6–10 fl oz).

Coupe
A stemmed glass with a broad, shallow bowl, previously and still used for Champagne and for shaken cocktails. Holds around 120–240 ml (4–8 fl oz).

Highball
A tall glass tumbler, usually holds 250–350 ml (8½–12 fl oz).

Martini Glass
Like a coupe, but V-shaped. Holds around 120 ml (4 fl oz) and is most famously used for martinis.

Rocks Glass
A short glass tumbler with a heavy glass base, used for cocktails that don't need much – or any – ice. Holds around 180–300 ml (6–10 fl oz).

Shot Glass
Just the right size for one measure, so 25 ml–50 ml (¾–1¾ fl oz). I've got an array of shot glasses at home, which are always good to have on hand for that time in the evening when friends want a Pickleback chaser (see page 127).

Blending

You'll find a bit of blending is needed when making the base pickle juices, shrubs and homemade ingredient recipes. Once you have these, it'll make creating the cocktails quick and easy.

Build

Building a cocktail is the easiest and quickest way to make one and involves adding each ingredient, one after the other, straight into the glass.

Muddling

Muddling is used to mash or press ingredients into the bottom of a glass to intensify their flavours.

Rimming

A lot of the Bloody Marys and some of the cocktails include rimming the glass with different seasonings. To do this, run a wedge of lemon or lime around the edge of the glass, making sure it is evenly coated in the juice. Prepare the seasoning and spread a thin layer onto a plate, then roll the rim of the glass in the seasoning so that it sticks to the juice (see photos on opposite page). This is a great way to add an extra dimension of flavour to a drink.

Shaking

Using a shaker, vigorously shake all the ingredients, slightly horizontally, with both hands for 10–15 seconds to aerate the cocktail. When making a sour cocktail, shaking creates that nice foaminess from the egg whites.

Sterilising

It is important to make sure all your jars and bottles are sterilised before using them, as this will ensure your recipes keep for much longer. The simplest and quickest way to sterilise glass jars or bottles is by putting them in a dishwasher. If you don't have one, heat your oven to 140°C (275°F/Gas 1). Wash your jars in hot soapy water, rinse well, then place on a baking tray and in the oven and leave until they're completely dry. If you're using Kilner jars, don't put the rubber seals in the oven, just wash then rinse with boiling water. Wash all jar lids with hot, soapy water then leave to dry, mouths facing up, on a clean tea towel.

Stirring

A lot of the cocktails will only need a stir using a bar spoon, which blends the ingredients and cools the drink.

Techniques

Sugars

Vinegars

Most vinegars work well in pickle juices and shrubs. My go-to is apple cider vinegar as it's smooth and blends well with most flavours, but you can also select a vinegar that will complement the other flavours in a drink. For example, a rice wine vinegar works well in a Vietnamese-style pickle juice, and a balsamic vinegar is great for a berry shrub – think strawberries and balsamic. When doing this, mix a small amount of your chosen vinegar with apple cider vinegar to avoid overpowering the fruit. I'd recommend:

> Apple cider vinegar with mother
>
> Balsamic vinegar
>
> Champagne vinegar
>
> Red wine vinegar
>
> Rice wine vinegar
>
> Sherry vinegar

Sugars

When it comes to pickling and making your own shrubs, I think it's worth playing around with the different sugars and vinegars to see how they work together with different fruits or vegetables. There are all sorts of sweeteners out there nowadays. A good old-fashioned white sugar (preferably unrefined) is great for vibrant flavours and colours; a light brown sugar adds depth of flavour; while nectars and syrups, such as agave and maple, make a good alternative. Here are a few I'd recommend:

> Agave nectar
>
> Coconut sugar
>
> Date syrup
>
> Demerara sugar
>
> Honey
>
> Light brown sugar
>
> Maple syrup

& Vinegars

Chickpea (garbanzos) Water

Chickpea water, also known as aquafaba, is the viscous liquid that comes from soaking or cooking beans in water. It's a great egg white substitute when making cocktails, as it creates the same silky foaminess while being vegan friendly. So next time you think about throwing away the water from a tin of chickpeas, think again and save it for your cocktails.

Fish Sauce, Tamarind Paste, Soy Sauce, Wasabi, Sriracha

These are all great flavour additions to a Bloody Mary. I wouldn't recommend putting them into a Bloody Mary all at once, but it's definitely worth trying a combination of a few.

Olive & Sesame Oil

Adding olive oil to a traditional Bloody Mary adds a really nice depth of flavour and texture, making it deliciously smooth to drink. Also try adding sesame oil to the Kimchi Bloody Mary (see page 78) for a similar effect.

Rice Flour

The rice flour is needed for the Kimchi recipe (see page 38) to create the thick glutinous porridge.

Sea Salt Flakes

Thin, light sea salt crystals, perfect for seasoning the rims of your cocktail glasses.

Smoked Water or Smoked Vodka

If you can get your hands on some smoked water or vodka, it makes for a delicious Bloody Mary. If not, Mezcal is also great for adding a hint of smokiness.

Tabasco

Tabasco is one of my all-time favourite hot sauces and can be used on absolutely anything. Having worked with their team in London, I later met Took, a fifth-generation family member of the McIlhenny Tabasco family. He taught me the lengthy process of how Tabasco is made and kept in barrels for a year to create the chilli mash. I love the simplicity of the ingredients yet how great the flavour is with no added nasties. A great addition to a Bloody Mary (see Pickle House Spice mix, page 70), your pickles or a Mango Shrub Margarita (see page 112) for a little extra kick.

Table Salt

Fine sea salt that is great for pickling as it dissolves a lot faster than other salts.

Worcestershire Sauce

There's the infamous Lea & Perrins, which is great, but there are also a few smaller craft ones that have come to market recently that are worth a try. Or, alternatively, make your own Vegan Worcestershire Sauce (see page 40).

Store-cupboard Ingredients

Allspice Berries
These look a little like peppercorns but have a similar aroma to a blend of clove, cinnamon and nutmeg. Make sure to remove these before serving.

Cayenne Pepper
Moderately hot and a great way to add heat to your pickle juice or shrubs. Cayenne pepper also helps improve blood circulation.

Celery Salt
Dried seasoning celery salt is a blend of salt and ground celery seeds. A great addition to a Bloody Mary and a really good seasoning for rimming glasses.

Coarsely Ground Black Pepper
I always go for coarsely ground black pepper over finely ground as I like the texture it adds to a drink, be it in a Bloody Mary (see Pickle House Spice Mix, page 70) or a Strawberry & Balsamic Shrub (see page 49) with a hint of black pepper.

Ground Cinnamon
I love the warming spiced flavour it adds to food and drinks. Definitely worth trying the Cinnamon & Apple Shrub (see page 61) for a more wintery cocktail.

Ground Turmeric
Yellow in colour, it adds a rich vibrancy to your pickle juice while also being packed full of antioxidants and having anti-inflammatory properties.

Hot Pepper Flakes
Be aware that hot pepper flakes are not the same as chilli flakes; they are much milder, so just be sure to taste before adding them to your Kimchi (see page 38) as you don't want to over-spice it.

Mustard seeds, Coriander seeds, Celery seeds
Great seeds to be adding to your pickles, as they each add their own intensity of flavour, which you can play around with depending on your preferences.

Old Bay
An American favourite, Old Bay seasoning is a blend of eighteen herbs and spices. I was introduced to this quite recently and now can't go without it. A great addition to Bloody Marys and a really good seasoning for rimming glasses.

Pul Biber (Aleppo pepper flakes)
I first discovered pul biber at my local newsagent. It's a Turkish pepper flake that's full of flavour with not too much heat.

Spices

Pickle juice

&

Shrubs

32

Pickle
juice

These recipes form the bases for all the cocktails in this book. They can be made in advance and kept in the refrigerator until needed. Once you've mastered the technique for pickling and shrub-making, you can then start to get more adventurous with your flavour combinations. Don't forget to eat the pickles – use them as cocktail garnishes and try the macerated fruits over yoghurt or ice cream.

Pickle Juice

This is a really good basic pickle juice, a great place to start if you're new to the pickling game. Once you've mastered this recipe, you can play around with different herbs and spices.

1 tablespoon white mustard seeds

1 teaspoon coriander seeds

1 teaspoon celery seeds

1 cucumber, sliced lengthways into 2.5 cm (1 in) sticks or 2 cm (¾ in) thick circles

few dashes of Tabasco

Pickling Juice

500 ml (17 fl oz/2 cups) water

500 ml (17 fl oz/2 cups) apple cider vinegar

1 teaspoon ground turmeric

2 tablespoons salt

5 tablespoons unrefined caster (superfine) sugar

Place the mustard seeds, coriander seeds and celery seeds in a sterilised Kilner jar (see page 23), or divide between 2 jars, depending on their size. Pack the jars as tightly as you can with the cucumbers.

Combine all the ingredients in a large saucepan for the pickling juice and heat slowly until everything has dissolved.

Using a funnel, pour the hot pickling juice into the jar. Make sure the juice covers the cucumbers, but leave about 1 cm (½ in) of room between the lid and the vinegar. Seal the jar, then leave them to cool for a couple of hours. Once cooled, refrigerate.

The pickles will be ready to eat the next day, but they're best left for 2 weeks before eating to mellow out the acidity of the vinegar, making the pickle juice smoother to drink. If you want something really special, don't touch them for up to 6 months. When making our Original Pickle Juice, we now leave the jars to sit for 1 year so the juices in the cucumber mellow out the acidity in the vinegar.

Spicy Dill Pickle

Makes 400 ml (13½ fl oz) or 16 × 25 ml (¾ fl oz) shots

Dill pickles remind me of New York and that first time I tried a Pickleback. Spice things up by adding some chillies and you've got yourself the perfect pickle juice for a Hot Smoked Chilliback (see page 127).

4 Lebanese (short baby) cucumbers, sliced in half lengthways

1 tablespoon coriander seeds

2 garlic cloves

2 red chillies, sliced in half lengthways

8 dill sprigs

1 tablespoon sugar

2 tablespoons sea salt flakes

150 ml (5 fl oz) distilled white wine vinegar

250 ml (8½ fl oz/1 cup) water

Put the baby cucumber in a sterilised Kilner jar (see page 23). Add the coriander seeds, garlic, chillies and dill.

Combine the sugar, salt and vinegar in a small saucepan over low heat and stir until the sugar and salt have dissolved. Remove from the heat and add the water, then pour into the jar, covering the cucumbers but leaving a 1 cm (½ in) gap between the lid and the brine.

Leave to cool for 2 hours, then seal the jar and refrigerate for at least 12 hours before eating.

From left to right: Sweet Vinegar, Kimchi Juice, Vegan Worcestershire Sauce, Pickle Juice and Carrot Pickle Juice

Kimchi to also make Kimchi juice

Makes 3 litres (101 fl oz)

My friend Jenny runs a Chinese supper club in London. We did a couple together – she did the food and I did the cocktails to go with her menu. My absolute favourite was the Kimchi Bloody Mary (see page 78), which is made using Jenny's kimchi recipe that she created after first being introduced to it in South Korea.

If you want to make it extra special, add some chopped squid at the same time you add the saeujot.

2 whole Chinese cabbages (wombok),
or white cabbages

315 g (11 oz/1 cup) table salt

1 bunch spring onions (scallions)

1 daikon (white radish) (if you can't
find daikon, use 4–5 radishes)

1 medium carrot

18 garlic cloves

½ large brown onion

5 cm (2 in) piece of ginger

60 ml (2 fl oz/¼ cup) fish sauce (see Note)

200 g (7 oz/2½ cups) Korean hot chilli flakes
(gochugaru)

1 tablespoon saeujot (a salted fermented
shrimp (prawn) that you can usually find in
Vietnamese and Chinese supermarkets
but if you can't find it, or want to keep it
vegan it's ok to leave it out)

Porridge

3 tablespoons sweet rice flour

750 ml (25½ fl oz/3 cups) water

3 tablespoons light brown sugar

Note

To make **Kimchi Juice**, follow the recipe
above and leave the kimchi to ferment
for 2 weeks. Blitz the kimchi in a blender
and strain through a fine-mesh sieve, then
drink the kimchi juice on its own, or use
it in cocktails, such as a Kimchi Bloody
Mary (see page 78). If you don't plan to
use it straight away, pour the juice into a
sterilised glass bottle (see page 23), seal
and refrigerate for up to 2 weeks.

To make a vegan substitute for fish sauce,
simply peel a ripe pineapple and blend
the flesh to a purée.

Cut the cabbage into bite-size pieces;
this will help speed up the salting
process. Place the cabbage in a large
bowl, cover with cold water, then add
the salt. Set aside for about 90 minutes,
turning the cabbage every 30 minutes to
ensure even salting. Drain and set aside.

While the cabbage is salting, make the
porridge. Combine the sweet rice flour
and water in a large saucepan over
medium heat. Stir for about 5 minutes,
or until a smooth glutinous paste forms.
Add the sugar and stir until dissolved,
then remove from the heat and set
aside to cool.

While the porridge is cooling, slice the
spring onions, daikon and carrot into
thin batons. In a food processor, blend
the garlic, onion and ginger until it
forms a paste.

Combine the cabbage, porridge, paste
and sliced vegetables in a large mixing
bowl, then add the fish sauce and chilli
flakes (add some extra chilli if you prefer
it really spicy). Squeeze the juices from
the saeujeot into the bowl, finely chop
the shrimp and add them to the mix.

Mix well, then transfer to a sterilised
airtight container or glass jar (see page
23) and leave to ferment for a couple
of days. To check on the fermenting
process, open the jar to see if it is
bubbling. If it isn't bubbling, leave it
for another day or two until it starts to
bubble and fizz.

Either eat it straight away (fresh kimchi
is lovely) or, if you have time, leave it for
2 weeks to ferment for the best results.

Vegan Worcestershire Sauce

**Makes 500 ml
(17 fl oz)**

This is a really simple recipe that can be made in advance and kept in the refrigerator. It may look like a lot of ingredients, but most of them are spices you may have lurking around the kitchen cupboard. I'm not vegan but have recently been trying to eat a lot less meat. It's also good to have an alternative to regular Worcestershire sauce when making Bloody Marys.

2 teaspoons olive oil

1 small white onion, chopped

2 teaspoons coarsely ground black pepper

2 teaspoons garlic powder

2 teaspoons ground ginger

3 tablespoons tamarind paste

½ teaspoon ground cinnamon

½ teaspoon ground allspice

170 g (6 oz) honey or agave nectar

150 ml (5 fl oz) water

4 tablespoons apple cider vinegar

1 teaspoon sea salt

2 tablespoons tomato paste

1 teaspoon cayenne pepper (or to taste)

Heat the olive oil in a frying pan (skillet) over low heat and sauté the onion until soft. Add the remaining ingredients and stir over low heat, then leave to simmer for about 30 minutes. This will allow the flavours to really blend together. Be sure to stir occasionally to prevent the sauce from sticking to the pan.

Strain the sauce through a fine-mesh sieve into a sterilised glass jar or bottle (see page 23). This is great in a Bloody Mary (see Pickle House Spice Mix, page 70), but also works well as an ingredient in marinades or dressings.

Pickled Tomato

Vodka

This was inspired by a pub lunch in Hackney, East London, where they had a huge jar filled with tomatoes, chillies and vodka sitting behind the bar. The bartender let us try a bit, which was amazing on its own and even better in a Bloody Mary.

20 cherry tomatoes (the better the quality the better the flavour)

1 tablespoon coriander seeds

1 tablespoon coarsely ground black pepper

1 teaspoon celery salt

4–6 dashes Tabasco (more if you like it spicy)

1 teaspoon Worcestershire sauce or Vegan Worcestershire Sauce (see page 40)

200 ml (7 fl oz) vodka (smoked vodka is even better if you have it)

Pickling Juice

100 ml (3½ fl oz) red wine vinegar

100 ml (3½ fl oz) apple cider vinegar

3 tablespoons salt

5 tablespoons light brown sugar

For the pickling juice, combine all the ingredients in a large saucepan and simmer over low heat until the salt and sugar have dissolved. Set aside to cool.

Meanwhile, prick the cherry tomatoes with a toothpick and place in a sterilised glass jar (see page 23). Add the coriander seeds, pepper, celery salt, Tabasco and Worcestershire sauce.

Pour the vodka into the pickling juice, give it a stir, then pour the mixture into the jar to completely cover the tomatoes. Seal the jar with a lid and store for up to 1 year unopened at room temperature.

Once opened, keep in the refrigerator for up to 1 month and use to make Deep Red (see page 86). The pickled cherry tomatoes can be used as a garnish.

Carrot Pickle Juice

This is a take on one of my favourite French salads, carottes râpées, or grated carrot salad. We used to eat it all the time when I was younger. My favourite part was drinking the juice that was leftover at the end… and here, we're making that juice! Using my French Granny's salad dressing, aka our Cherruault family dressing, but with a few slight changes, this is great on its own or as an addition to cocktails.

5 carrots, grated

Dressing

1 teaspoon Dijon mustard

4 tablespoons olive oil

2 tablespoons lemon juice

½ teaspoon sea salt

pinch of freshly cracked black pepper

To make the dressing, whisk the mustard and oil in a large mixing bowl, then add the lemon juice, salt and pepper and mix well. The dressing shouldn't be too thick, and should be thin enough to dress the carrots evenly (see Note).

Add the grated carrots to the bowl and mix, making sure the carrots are well coated in the dressing. Cover with cling film (plastic wrap) and leave in the refrigerator overnight.

The next day, you'll notice there's a good amount of juice at the bottom of the bowl. At this point, you can simply eat the carrots and store the juice. Or, if you're like me and prefer the juice, blend the salad and strain through a piece of muslin (cheesecloth). Using a funnel, pour the juice into a sterilised glass bottle (see page 23) and keep in your refrigerator for up to 1 month.

Note

All olive oils, vinegars and mustards are slightly different in texture and taste, so be sure to taste them first before combining.

Sweet Vietnamese Vinegar

Makes 150 ml (5 fl oz)

Drinking sweet vinegar is something I discovered really recently and, oh man, I could drink it on its own every day. I was out for dinner with my boyfriend and we had a fried chicken dish that came with a sweet vinegar dipping sauce. Let's just say, it was never used for dipping as we sipped most of it before the chicken got a look-in. This recipe is my take on the one we tried.

2 tablespoon honey

4 tablespoons warm water

60 ml (2 fl oz/¼ cup) rice wine vinegar

1 teaspoon light soy sauce

1 thumb-size piece of ginger, grated

Mix all the ingredients together in a small bowl until the honey has dissolved.

Pour the vinegar into a sterilised glass bottle (see page 23) and keep in your refrigerator for up to 1 month.

This is a great alternative drink if you find a Pickleback (see page 127) too intense.

Shrubs, also known as drinking vinegars, are one of my all-time favourite things. They are made of fruit or vegetables combined with sugar and vinegar to form a concentrated syrup. They have the right amount of sweetness with a nice touch of acidity from the vinegar and are best served over ice topped up with soda water (club soda) or as an addition to cocktails.

Shrubs

The

Traditional Shrub Method

This is my preferred method of making shrubs, but it does take a couple of days for the fruit or vegetables to macerate with the sugar. What's great about shrubs is that once you've got the ratios sorted for fruit, sugar and vinegar, you can get creative and start putting together really interesting flavours.

When making shrubs, I find it much easier to measure everything in cups rather than weighing the ingredients on the scales. For the traditional method use a 2:1:1 ratio, so 2 cups of fruit or vegetables to 1 cup of sugar and 1 cup of vinegar. Macerate the fruit or vegetable in the sugar over night, strain then add the vineger

You can also play around with different vinegars and sugars (see page 24) for different tastes and textures. Here are a few of my favourite shrubs, which I'll then show you how to use in cocktails.

Cucumber shrub

Makes 400 ml
(13½ fl oz)

Cucumbers make the most refreshing shrub and are great all year round. This shrub is especially good when added to a gin and tonic.

1 whole cucumber, diced
(about 2 cups)

1 cup unrefined caster
(superfine) sugar

1 cup apple cider vinegar,
with the mother

Put the diced cucumber in a bowl and scatter over the sugar. Mix well, making sure the sugar coats all of the cucumber. Cover the bowl with cling film (plastic wrap) and leave in the refrigerator or a cool place for 48 hours. Stir occasionally to make sure all the sugar dissolves.

Strain the cucumber through a fine-mesh sieve into a bowl. If you have a piece of muslin (cheesecloth), strain the cucumber through this as well to extract all its juices.

Add the vinegar to the cucumber syrup and mix well, then pour it into a sterilised glass jar or bottle (see page 23), seal with a lid and refrigerate. You can use it straight away, but I find it tastes much better after a week once the flavours have had a chance to combine.

Strawberry & Balsamic Shrub

**Makes 400 ml
(13½ fl oz)**

Strawberries are great for shrubs, as they quickly create a syrup when macerated with sugar, so don't necessarily need to be left for the full 48 hours.

2 cups diced strawberries
(about half a punnet)

1 cup unrefined caster
(superfine) sugar

1 cup apple cider vinegar with
the mother

1 tablespoon balsamic vinegar

Combine the strawberries with the sugar in a bowl, then cover with cling film (plastic wrap) and set aside overnight at room temperature to macerate. The next day, give the strawberries a stir to make sure all the sugar has dissolved.

For strawberries, I like to use a piece of muslin (cheesecloth) for straining to make sure none of the seeds end up in the shrub. Add the vinegars and mix well. If you prefer a slightly less acidic shrub, add the vinegars gradually, tasting as you go, to achieve the right balance.

Pour into a sterilised glass bottle (see page 23), seal with a lid and store in the refrigerator for up to 1 month.

Note

Add a pinch of coarsely ground black pepper for a little hint of spice.

If you have a juicer this is a great way to make a quick shrub that's ready to drink instantly.

Quick

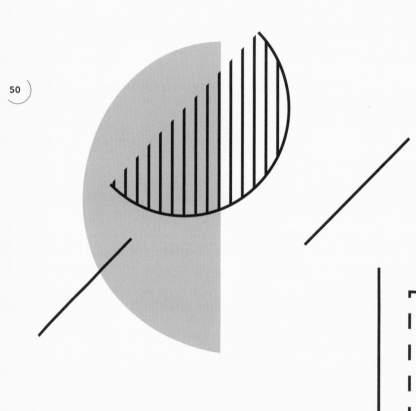

Shrub

When you're strapped for time but still fancy that sweet vinegary goodness you can make a quick shrub with the help of a juicer or fruits with a high water content. The results from using this method are much less of a cordial texture and uses less sugar so you can add more shrub into your drink to be mixed with sparkling water. The basic quick method is as follows: use a juicer to juice the fruit then add sugar syrup and vinegar. Or use fruit with a high water content and mush it through a sieve to get the juice then add sugar syrup and vinegar. It's that easy.

Method

Beetroot & Apple Shrub

**Makes 400 ml
(13½ fl oz)**

If you have a juicer, this recipe is great for making a quick shrub that's ready to drink straight away.

The earthy tones of beetroot work really well with the vinegar, creating a vibrant shrub full of flavour. I've added apple to this recipe, which gives it an extra note of sweetness, but beetroot on its own is also just as good.

50 ml (1¾ fl oz) juiced beetroot

50 ml (1¾ fl oz) juiced apple

25 ml (¾ fl oz) apple cider vinegar

15 ml (½ fl oz) sugar syrup
(see below)

Sugar Syrup (see Note)

230 g (8 oz/2 cups) unrefined caster (superfine) sugar

250 ml (8½ fl oz/1 cup) water

To make the sugar syrup, combine the sugar and water in a saucepan over low heat and heat gently until the sugar dissolves. Set aside to cool while you juice the apple and beetroot.

Mix the beetroot and apple juices in a bowl, then add the vinegar and 15 ml (½ fl oz) of sugar syrup. (I'm a big fan of the tartness of the vinegar, but if you'd prefer it a bit sweeter you can add a little more sugar syrup.) And voila!

Pour into a sterilised glass bottle or a jar (see page 23), seal with a lid and you have your beetroot and apple shrub. Store in the refrigerator for up to 1 month.

Note

Make more sugar syrup than you need by doubling, or even tripling the recipe, and store in a sealed sterilised glass jar or bottle in the cupboard for another day. It will keep for up to 1 year.

Watermelon Shrub

Makes 600 ml (20½ fl oz)

Watermelons are ideal for making a quick shrub because of their high water content. This is a good go-to shrub when you're in a hurry, as it doesn't need much time to macerate.

400 g (14 oz) watermelon

125 ml (4 fl oz/½ cup) white wine vinegar

100 ml (3½ fl oz) water

25 g (1 oz) granulated sugar

15 ml (½ fl oz) lemon juice

3 allspice berries

1 teaspoon salt

1 teaspoon cayenne pepper

Remove the skin and seeds from the watermelon and cut the flesh into small pieces. Place the watermelon in a mixing bowl and add the remaining ingredients.

Using a fork, mash up the watermelon to make sure it blends with all the other ingredients. Cover with cling film (plastic wrap) and set aside for about 1 hour.

After an hour, give it a stir to make sure the sugar and salt have dissolved. Strain through a piece of muslin (cheesecloth) into a bowl, then transfer to a sterilised glass jar or bottle (see page 23), seal with a lid and store in the refrigerator for up to 1 month.

Note

Add a pinch of coarsely ground black pepper for a little hint of spice.

From left to right: Strawberry Shrub, Cucumber Shrub, Cinnamon & Apple Shrub, Beetroot & Apple Shrub, Blackberry & Fresh Thyme Shrub, Watermelon Shrub, Mango Shrub

Heated shrubs are great if you're short on time as they're simply made by heating all the ingredients then straining through a fine-mesh sieve before cooling and storing. For heated shrubs, I'd recommend using raspberries, strawberries, blackcurrants or apples, essentially any fruit that can be enjoyed hot. For example, I wouldn't recommend making a heated watermelon shrub. The basic heated method uses 2 of cups fruit, 1 of cup sugar and 1 of cup vinegar. Put the sugar in a pan with the fruit and heat until it has all mixed together then add the vinegar. Allow to cool, strain and bottle!

Heated

Shrub

Method

Raspberry Shrub

**Makes 500 ml
(17 fl oz)**

1 cup unrefined caster
(superfine) sugar

1 cup water

150 g (5 oz) raspberries

1 cup Champagne vinegar
or apple cider vinegar

Combine the sugar and water in a
saucepan over medium heat and stir
until the sugar has dissolved.

Add the raspberries and simmer over low
heat until the raspberries break down and
blend with the water and sugar.

Add the vinegar and simmer for another
couple of minutes to allow the flavours
to marry together. Set aside to cool,
then strain through a fine-mesh sieve to
separate the raspberry solids.

Pour into a sterilised glass jar or bottle
(see page 23) and store in the refrigerator
for up to 1 month.

A heated raspberry shrub works really nicely. The heating
process allows the raspberries to break down and blend
with the sugar as it dissolves, creating a sort of raspberry
jam, which is then mixed with vinegar.

Oleo-saccharum

OK so technically not a shrub, but I discovered this recipe when I first started making them. Oleo-saccharum basically means 'oil sugar' and refers to the process of extracting oil from citrus peel. Reknowned for its use in punch, oleo-saccharum can also be added to shrubs and is a great addition if you want to add a citrusy note. The photo shows the process for making a Lemon Oleo-saccharum.

citrus peel from 1 orange,
1 grapefruit or 2 lemons
(for every 1 cup sugar)

1 cup unrefined sugar
(or use the measurements in
the shrub recipe you're using)

Remove the peel from the citrus fruit, making sure not to take off too much of the pith (see Note). Combine the peel and sugar in a bowl. Use your fingers to massage the sugar into the peel, squeezing out the oils from the peel as you go. Cover with cling film (plastic wrap) and set aside for about 1 hour to allow the flavour to develop.

After an hour, remove the peel and your oleo-saccharum is ready to be used. Add it to any of your shrubs in place of the normal sugar. Store in a sealed airtight container in the refridgerator for up to 1 month.

If you like sharp flavours, I would highly recommend making a Lemon Shrub (see page 61) using lemon oleo-saccharum. It's really refreshing and a great addition to cocktails.

Note

Once you have removed the peel from your citrus fruit, don't throw the fruit away. Keep it to make a citrus shrub, like the Lemon Shrub on page 61.

Lemon Shrub

**Makes 200 ml
(7 fl oz)**

2 lemons

1 cup Lemon Oleo-saccharum
(see page 58)

1 cup apple cider vinegar

Dice the lemons then combine in a bowl with the oleo-saccharum. Cover with cling film (plastic wrap) and leave in the refrigerator or a cool place for 48 hours, stirring occasionally.

Strain the contents through a fine-mesh sieve into a bowl, discarding the solids. If you have a piece of muslin (cheesecloth), strain the mixture a second time to extract as much juice as possible.

Add the vinegar to the lemon syrup and mix well, then pour into a sterilised glass jar or bottle (see page 23), seal and refrigerate for up to 1 month. You can use it straight away, but I find it tastes much better after a week once the flavours have combined.

Cinnamon & Apple Shrub

**Makes 500 ml
(17 fl oz/2 cups)**

Apple and cinnamon is such a great combination as a purée, and it's just as good in a shrub. This is the perfect wintery shrub and, if you want to make it extra special, try adding some allspice berries to the mix.

1 cup water

1 cup unrefined caster (superfine) sugar

2 cups diced apple (green or cooking apples work well)

1 teaspoon ground cinnamon

1 cup apple cider vinegar

Combine the water, sugar, apple and cinnamon in a saucepan over medium heat and cook for around 5 minutes, giving it a stir occasionally.

Once all the ingredients have blended and the apple has gone soft (you want the mixture to blend into a purée), add the vinegar and simmer for another couple of minutes.

Set aside to cool, then strain through a piece of muslin (cheesecloth) and pour into a sterilised glass jar or bottle (see page 23). Store in the refrigerator for up to 1 month.

Other Shrub Flavours I Like

Strawberry & Basil
(Traditional or Quick Shrub Method, pages 47 or 51)

Rhubarb
(Traditional or Heated Shrub Method, pages 47 or 51)

Orange
(Traditional or Quick Shrub Method, page 47 or 51)

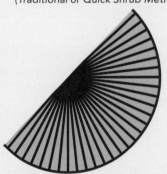

Pineapple
(Traditional Shrub Method, page 47)

Blackberry & Fresh Thyme
(Heated Shrub Method, page 56)

Mango & Black Pepper
(Traditional or Quick Shrub Method, pages 47 or 51)

Apple
(Traditional Shrub Method, page 47)

Beetroot
(Quick Shrub Method, page 51)

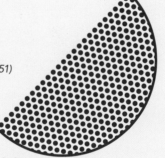

ango & Ginger
ditional or Quick Shrub Method, pages 47 or 51)

Cucumber, Lime & Mint
(Traditional or Quick Shrub Method, pages 47 or 51)

Pink Grapefruit Shrub
(Traditional or Quick Shrub Method, pages 47 or 51)

Raspberry & Lemon Shrub
(Make the Oleo-saccharum using a lemon on page 58 and then mix with raspberries and make using Traditional Shrub Method on page 47)

Bloody

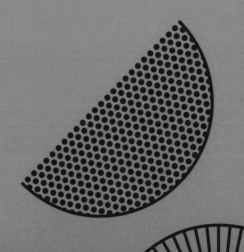

Mary

66

Much like the Pickleback, the origin of the Bloody Mary is a little unclear. Fernand Petiot, a French bartender who was working at the New York Bar in Paris, claims to have invented the Bloody Mary in 1921, while Henri Zbikiewics is said to have mixed the first Bloody Mary in the 1930s in New York's 21 Club. I wasn't around back then, but my first memory of a Bloody Mary was of my mum religiously ordering one whenever she went on a flight (and I can definitely say she didn't invent the Bloody Mary).

From top left, clockwise: Kimchi Bloody Mary, Michelada,
Verde Maria, Summer Bloody Mary, Deep Red and Pickle
House Snapper by Hawksmoor

Pickle House Spice Mix

Makes 60 ml
(2 fl oz)

This spice mix can be made in advance so it's on hand for those mornings when you really need a Bloody Mary pick-me-up.

80 ml (2¾ fl oz) Pickle Juice
(see page 34)

2 tablespoon Worcestershire
sauce or Vegan Worcestershire
Sauce (see page 40)

2 teaspoon grated (or
creamed) horseradish

1 teaspoon celery salt

2 teaspoon coarsely ground
black pepper

a few dashes of Tabasco

Combine all the ingredients in a bowl, then transfer to a sterilised glass bottle (see page 23) using a funnel.

Store in the refrigerator for up to 2 weeks. If you don't add the horseradish, this spice mix will keep for up to 1 year.

Original Bloody Mary

This Bloody Mary mix can be used as the base for all Bloody Marys. Try other versions by replacing the vodka with gin to make a Red Snapper, with tequila for a Bloody Maria, or with Mezcal to add a nice smokiness.

30 ml (1 fl oz) vodka

125 ml (4 fl oz/½ cup) good-quality tomato juice

25 ml (¾ fl oz) Pickle Juice (see page 34)

1 tablespoon Pickle House Spice Mix (see page 70)

ice cubes, to serve

cucumber slice and pul biber (Aleppo pepper flakes), to garnish

Build the ingredients over ice in a highball glass, starting with the vodka, then the tomato juice, followed by the pickle juice and spice mix. Stir thoroughly.

Garnish with a cucumber slice and a sprinkling of pul biber.

Fiery

When a friend of mine who also helps out with The Pickle House first told me about this mix he'd concocted, I was a little dubious. But after a night of mixing cocktails and testing them out for this book, it was a clear winner. Make sure you use a really strong fiery ginger ale.

35 ml (1¼ fl oz) whisky

75 ml (2½ fl oz) dry fiery ginger ale

125 ml (4 fl oz/½ cup) Original Bloody Mary (see opposite)

ice cubes, to serve

mint leaf, to garnish

Build all the ingredients over ice in a rocks glass, starting with the whisky, then the ginger beer and finally the Bloody Mary.

Stir thoroughly and garnish with a mint leaf.

Ginger Mary

Pickle House Snapper by Hawksmoor

Hawksmoor in London was one of the first bars to serve my pickle juice. Bloody Marys made with gin are known as Red Snappers, and the gin adds a really nice flavour to the mix.

15 ml (½ fl oz) gin

15 ml (½ fl oz) Pickle Juice
(see page 34)

15 ml (½ fl oz) Kamm & Sons
(optional)

5 ml (⅛ fl oz) lemon juice

125 ml (4 fl oz/½ cup) tomato juice

1 teaspoon Pickle House Spice Mix
(see page 70)

ice cubes, to serve

pul biber (Aleppo pepper flakes),
for rimming

Build the ingredients over ice in a rocks glass rimmed with pul biber (see Note), starting with the gin, then the pickle juice, followed by the Kamm & Sons (if using), lemon juice, tomato juice and spice mix. Stir thoroughly and serve.

Note

See the best way to rim your glass on pages 22–23.

From left to right: Pickle House Snapper and Michelada

Michelada

A refreshingly light version of a Bloody Mary, Micheladas are great all year round but make the perfect accompaniment to a summer barbecue.

50 ml (2 fl oz) Original Bloody Mary (see page 72)

1 x 355 ml (12 fl oz) bottle light Mexican beer (I like to use Modelo)

juice of ½ lime

ice cubes, to serve

lime wedge, red chilli and olive, to garnish

Chilli Lime Salt

zest of ½ lime

1 teaspoon sea salt flakes

½ teaspoon Old Bay seasoning or mild chilli powder

To make the chilli lime salt, combine all the ingredients in a small bowl and rim a rocks glass (see page 23).

Build the ingredients over ice in the glass, starting with the Bloody Mary, then the beer and lime juice. Stir thoroughly.

Garnish with a lime wedge, chilli and olive.

Serve any leftover beer alongside the cocktail for topping up.

Verde Maria

I made this cocktail for an event we did with Pantone and Airbnb. They'd turned a house in London into a beautiful inside-out garden house and wanted a green Bloody Mary for the event. This one's also just as good without the booze.

25 ml (¾ fl oz) white rum

25 ml (¾ fl oz) green chilli liqueur

125 ml (4 fl oz) Maria Mix (see below)

ice cubes, to serve

lime wedge, avocado slice, cornichon and rosemary sprig, to garnish

Maria Mix

1 cucumber, peeled and deseeded

6 coriander (cilantro) sprigs

50 ml (2 fl oz) Pickle Juice (see page 34)

1 green pepper (bell pepper)

juice of ½ lime

1 celery stalk

pinch of ground cumin

pinch of celery salt

pinch of ground coriander

pinch of coarsely ground black pepper

100 ml (3½ fl oz) water

10 dashes green Tabasco

To make the Maria mix, combine all the ingredients in a blender and blend to a purée. Pass the mixture through a piece of muslin (cheesecloth) into a bowl.

Build the ingredients over ice in a rocks glass, starting with the rum, then the green chilli liqueur and finally the Maria mix.

Stir thoroughly, then garnish with a lime wedge, a slice of avocado, cornichon and a sprig of rosemary.

Kimchi

I first made this for my friend's supper club. The kimchi juice and sesame oil really make this Mary. I'd highly recommend putting the effort into making the Kimchi (see page 38) for this, but if you are stuck for time a store-bought one will work fine.

75 ml (2½ fl oz) good-quality tomato juice

30 ml (1 fl oz) Kimchi Juice (see page 38)

juice of ½ lime

1 teaspoon sesame oil

1 teaspoon Sriracha (or more if you like it hotter)

ice cubes, to serve

50 ml (2 fl oz) vodka

Kimchi (page 38) and shredded nori, to garnish

Stir together the tomato juice, kimchi juice, lime juice, sesame oil and Sriracha.

Build over ice with the vodka in a highball glass. Stir thoroughly.

Garnish with kimchi and pieces of nori.

Bloody Mary

Very Dirty Mary

When they say dirty, they mean dirty! This Mary is packed full of flavour, with the Pringle rim adding that extra bit of *je ne sais quoi*.

50 ml (2 fl oz) vodka

75 ml (2½ fl oz) tomato juice

10 ml (¼ fl oz) Pickle Juice (see page 34)

10 ml (¼ fl oz) Belsazar red vermouth

½ teaspoon wasabi

½ teaspoon Sriracha

pinch of coarsely ground black pepper

½ teaspoon Chilli Lime Salt (see page 75)

½ teaspoon ketchup

ice cubes, to serve

crushed salted Pringles, for rimming

Grilled Cheese Toastie (page 83), to garnish

celery stalk and cornichon, to garnish

Build all the ingredients over ice in a rocks or highball glass rimmed with crushed Pringles in the order listed. Stir thoroughly.

Make your grilled cheese toastie according to the method on page 83.

Serve with a celery stalk and half a cheese toastie.

Note

See rimming technique on pages 22–23.

by Dirty Bones

Quick Grilled Cheese Toastie

for the Dirty Mary

What is great on a hangover? A Bloody Mary and anything beige. So what better way to help you out than merging those two things together and garnishing your Mary with a deliciously gooey and crispy grilled cheese toastie. Yum!

Makes enough to garnish 4 Dirty Mary

1 tablespoon butter

2 slices of thick (about 1cm/½ in) sliced white bread

50 g (2 oz/¼ cup) Cheddar cheese, grated

Butter each slice of bread on both sides, then pile the grated cheese onto one of the slices and close the sandwich with the other.

Heat up a frying pan (skillet) on a medium heat. Once hot, place the sandwich in the pan and fry for 2–3 minutes on each side until golden brown and crisp. Press some weight down onto the bread to make sure the cheese melts and that there's a nice golden brown colour to the bread.

Place on a chopping board and cut into 4 quarters. Using a wooden skewer, pierce through the centre of each piece and place on top of your Dirty Mary, using the sides of the glass to help it balance.

Note

You can also mix it up and add in a bit of red Leicester.

To elevate your toastie, add 4 slices of pickled cucumber from Pickle Juice recipe on page 34.

From left to right: Pickle House Snapper by Hawksmoor,
Kimchi Bloody Mary, Michelada, Deep Red (also far right),
Verde Maria and Summer Bloody Mary

Summer Bloody Mary

This refreshing Bloody Mary uses fresh tomato juice and makes a great alternative during the hotter months.

4–6 tomatoes

50 ml (2 fl oz) Pickled Tomato Vodka (see page 42)

1–2 tomatoes (from the Pickled Tomato Vodka) on a toothpick, to garnish

freshly ground black pepper, to garnish

Note

Every tomato varies in size so you may need to use more or fewer tomatoes depending on their size.

Blend the tomatoes to a fine purée. Strain through a piece of muslin (cheesecloth). You should end up with around 150 ml (5 fl oz) of tomato juice (see Note).

Build the remaining ingredients with the tomato juice in a rocks glass. Stir thoroughy and garnish with pickled tomatoes and a grinding of black pepper.

Both serve 1

Deep Red

35 ml (1¼ fl oz) vodka

20 ml (¾ fl oz) Strawberry & Balsamic Shrub (see page 49)

50 ml (2 fl oz) red wine

5 ml (⅛ fl oz) lemon juice

ice cubes, to serve

rosemary spring, to garnish

freshly ground black pepper, to garnish

This may seem like a weird one, but if you've got the Strawberry & Balsamic Shrub (see page 49) hanging out in your refrigerator, try this red wine Bloody Mary. The red wine gives it depth and dryness, while the strawberry shrub counteracts all of that with a fresh sweetness.

Build all the ingredients over ice in a rocks glass in the order listed. Stir and garnish with the rosemary sprig and a grinding of black pepper.

Cocktails &

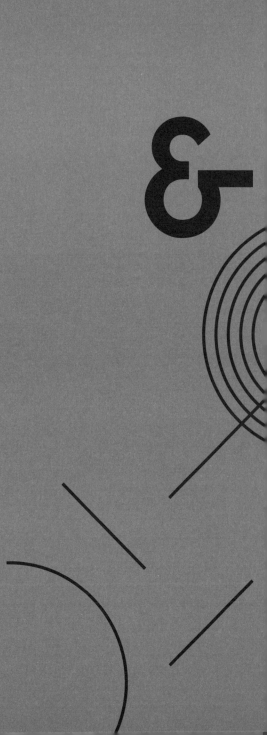

Chasers

Cocktails

Adding pickle juice and shrubs to your cocktails is a bit of a game changer; they add this really delicious umami flavour, which puts a different spin on the usually sweet cocktail. What's great is that they can be added to non-alcoholic cocktails too (see pages 132–147), with the sharp tang from the vinegar adding depth and complexity to a drink. You can easily omit the alcohol from any of these drinks, if you fancy going T-total – it's up to you. They will still taste great!

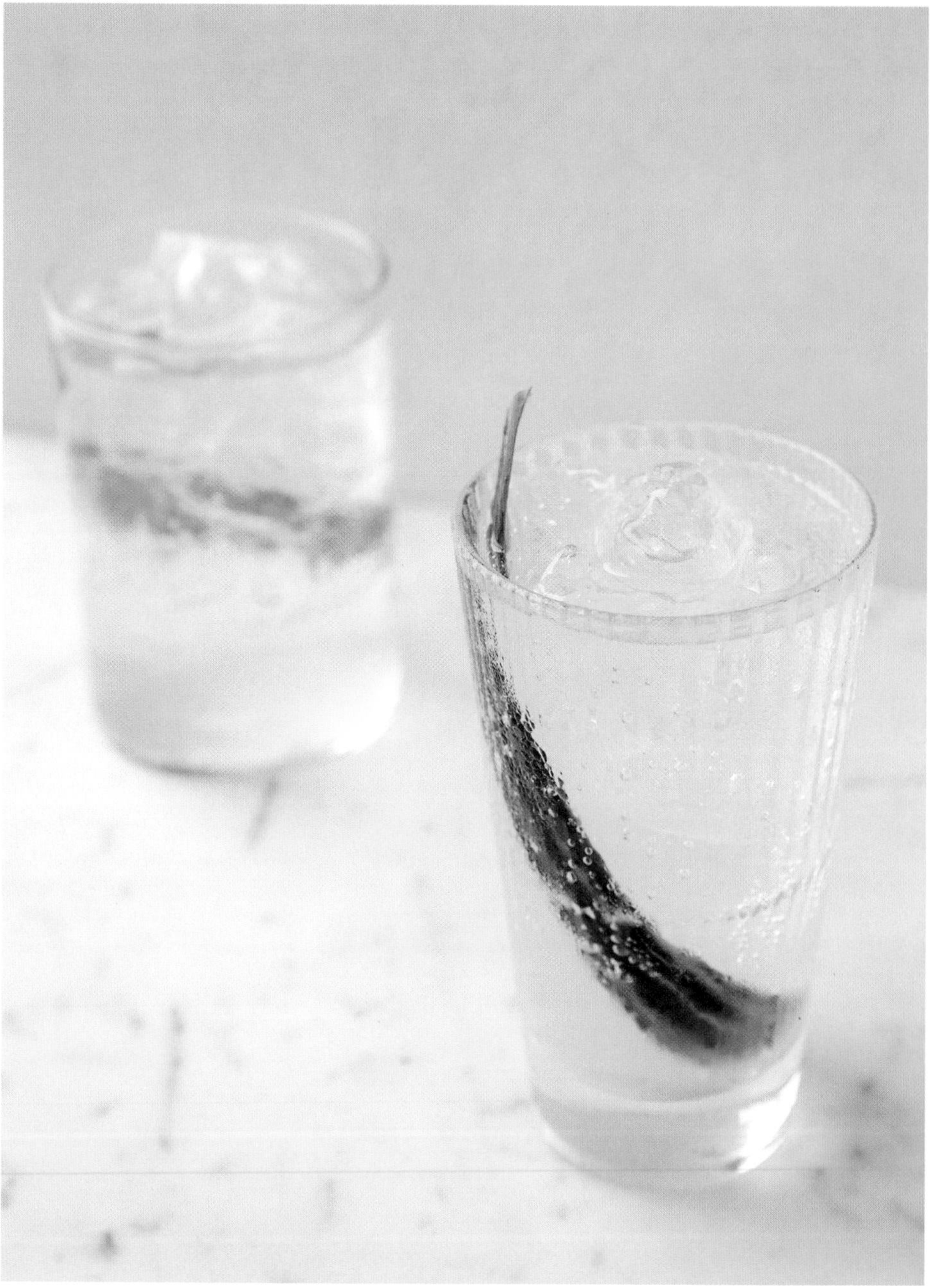

25 ml (¾ fl oz) Cucumber Shrub
(see page 48)

30 ml (1 fl oz) gin

100 ml (3½ fl oz) tonic water

ice cubes, to serve

cucumber ribbon, to garnish

Build the ingredients over ice,
starting with the cucumber
shrub followed by the gin and
tonic water.

Slightly twist the cucumber ribbon
and allow it to swirl around inside
the glass, before drinking.

Pickle House G & T

A refreshing twist for lovers of a G&T with cucumber.
This is the perfect cocktial for a summers evening but
actually, let's be honest, it can be enjoyed all year round.

Serves 1

15 ml (½ fl oz) Mango Shrub
(see Note)

125 ml (4 fl oz/½ cup) prosecco
or Champagne

lemon slice, to garnish

Pour the mango shrub into the
bottom of your Champagne
flute. Pop open the prosecco
and pour into the glass, slowly.

Make sure you do this slowly as
the mango shrub will react with
the Champagne and make it
fizz more then usual.

Note

Make the shrub using the
traditional shrub method on
page 47, using 2 cups of diced
mango. It will make more shrub
than required for this recipe,
but store it in a sterilised
jar (see page 23) and keep
refrigerated for up to 1 month.
This is also great to use in the
Mango Shrub Margarita on
page 112.

Tro-Pickle Fizz

A great addition to brunch or a summer lunch or a
celebratory dinner or party, the Tro-Pickle Fizz is kind
of like the pickled sister of a mimosa.

50 ml (2 fl oz) white rum

30 ml (1 fl oz) Rhubarb Shrub
(see Note)

juice of ½ lime (approx.
25 ml/¾ fl oz lime juice)

ice cubes, for shaking

3 green apple slices, to garnish

Combine all the ingredients in
a cocktail shaker with the ice and
shake vigorously for 10 seconds.

Strain into a coupe glass and
garnish with apple slices.

Note

Make the shrub using the
heated shrub method on page
51. It will make more shrub
than required for this recipe,
but store it in a sterilised
jar (see page 23) and keep
refrigerated for up to 1 month.

Pickled Rhuby Daiquiri

When rhubarb is in season there's always so much of it,
so making a rhubarb shrub is a great way to use it up.
This rhuby daiquiri has a really nice sweet and zingy flavour.

Serves 1

25 ml (¾ fl oz) Ginger Shrub (see Note)

25 ml (¾ fl oz) Cucumber Shrub (see page 49)

50 ml (2 fl oz) rum

juice of ½ lime (approx. 25 ml/¾ fl oz lime juice)

ice cubes, for shaking and serving

red chilli and rosemary sprig, to garnish

Combine all the ingredients in a cocktail shaker with the ice and shake vigorously for 10 seconds.

Strain into a rocks glass filled with ice cubes.

Cut the end of the chilli off and use to stir the drink to add more spice, then garnish with tthe top end of the sliced chilli and the rosemary sprig.

Note

Make the shrub using the heated shrub method on page 51. It will make more shrub than required for this recipe, but store it in a sterilised jar (see page 23) and keep refrigerated for up to 1 month.

Cucumber & Ginger Shrub

Cucumber and ginger go hand-in-hand, being both refreshing and fiery at the same time. This cocktail is great all year round but is especially good during the colder months when you're in need of a bit of extra heat!

25 ml (¾ fl oz) Strawberry
& Balsamic Shrub (see page 49)

50 ml (2 fl oz) rum

juice of ½ lime (approx.
25 ml/¾ fl oz lime juice)

ice cubes, for shaking

crushed ice, to serve

macerated strawberries
(from the shrub), to garnish

Combine all the ingredients
in a cocktail shaker with
the ice and shake vigorously
for 10 seconds.

Strain into a coupe glass
filled with crusshed ice, and
garnish with a few macerated
strawberries.

Serves 1

Frozen Strawberry
Shrub Daiquiri

Deliciously refreshing, this drink will take you straight back
to THAT summer holiday.

30 ml (1 fl oz) vodka

15 ml (½ fl oz) Pickle Juice
(see page 34)

100 ml (3½ fl oz) ginger ale

ice cubes, to serve

very thin slice of lime, to garnish

Build all the ingredients over
ice in rocks glass, starting with
the vodka, then pickle juice and
finishing with the ginger ale.

Stir, then carefully top your drink
with the sliced lime and enjoy.

Serves 1

Note

Make sure you slice the lime
as finely as possible so it floats
nicely on top of your drink.

In a Pickle

This is one of the first cocktails I ever made with pickle
juice, and it has always been a great hit with people trying
pickle juice for the first time.

35 ml (1¼ fl oz) Hendrick's gin

15 ml (½ fl oz) St Germain elderflower liqueur (alternatively can use elderflower cordial)

10 ml (¼ fl oz) Pickle Juice (see page 34)

dash of egg white, or substitute with chickpea (garbanzos) water (aquafaba) to make it vegan

1 teaspoon lime juice

ice cubes, for shaking

8 mint leaves, plus 1 mint leaf, to garnish

Muddle all the ingredients in a cocktail shaker until the juices release.

Top with ice, then seal and shake vigorously for 10 seconds.

Strain into a martini glass and garnish with a mint leaf.

Serves 1

La Soirée by Ping Pong

I love most things with elderflower, and if you're feeling a little adventurous about using egg white in your cocktails, this one makes a light, sweet and savoury drink.

Serves 1

25 ml (¾ fl oz) gin

25 ml (¾ fl oz) vodka

25 ml (¾ fl oz) Lillet Blanc

5 ml (⅛ fl oz) Pickle Juice
(see page 34)

ice cubes, for shaking

cornichon, to garnish

Pickle Vesper

Combine all the ingredients in a
cocktail shaker, top with ice and
shake vigorously for 10 second.

Strain into a martini glass
and garnish with a cornichon.

My dad's a big fan of vespers and a hint of pickle juice
gives it a nice savoury kick.

50 ml (2 fl oz) vodka

10 ml (¼ fl oz) good-quality
dry vermouth

5 ml (⅛ fl oz) Pickle Juice
(see page 34)

ice cubes, for shaking

lemon twist, to garnish

Serves 1

Combine all the ingredients
in a cocktail shaker, top with
ice and shake vigorously for
10 seconds.

Strain into a martini glass and
garnish with a lemon twist.

Dirty Pickle Martini

Similar to the vesper, this is a pickled take on a Dirty Martini.
In my opinion it tastes even better then the classic ... don't
believe me? Then give it a go!

From left to right: Le Boulevesant by Sketch,
Pickle Sour and Watermelon Shrub Sour

Serves 1

25 ml (¾ fl oz) bourbon

15 ml (½ fl oz) Aperol

15 ml (½ fl oz) Belsazar dry
vermouth

15 ml (½ fl oz) Pickle Juice
(see page 34)

1 teaspoon maple syrup

ice cubes, for shaking

1 dash Tabasco and Burlesque
bitters, to garnish

Le Boulevesant
by Sketch

Combine all the ingredients in a
cocktail shaker, top with ice and
shake vigorously for 10 seconds.

Strain into a coupe glass and
garnish with a dash of Tabasco
and Burlesque bitters.

A good sipping cocktail to take your time over.

50 ml (2 fl oz) vodka

15 ml (½ fl oz) Pickle Juice
(see page 34)

15 ml (½ fl oz) lemon juice

15 ml (½ fl oz) Sugar Syrup
(see page 52)

2 dashes Angostura bitters

handful of mint leaves
(approx. 8 leaves)

ice cubes, for shaking

crushed ice, to serve

lemon peel, to garnish

Combine all the ingredients
in a cocktail shaker, top with
ice and shake vigorously for
10 seconds.

Strain into a coupe glass over
crushed ice and garnish with
a lemon peel.

Pickle Sour

A light, summery cocktail and a great example of pickle juice
adding that savoury-sweet depth of flavour.

50 ml (2 fl oz) gin

20 ml (¾ fl oz) Watermelon
Shrub (see page 53)

dash of egg white, or substitute
with chickpea (garbanzos) water
(aquafaba) to make it vegan

ice cubes, for shaking

watermelon seeds, to garnish

Serves 1

Combine the ingredients
in a cocktail shaker,
top with ice and shake
vigorously for 10 seconds.

Strain into a coupe glass
and garnish with a a few
watermelon seeds.

Watermelon Shrub Sour

To create that nice foam on cocktails you'll need egg whites,
but I discovered recently that the water (aquafaba) in a tin of
chickpeas (garbanzos) works just as well if you'd like a vegan
option (see page 26).

Serves 1

25 ml (¾ fl oz) Raspberry Shrub
(see page 57)

40 ml (1¼ fl oz) Pisco

20 ml (¾ fl oz) lemon juice

1 small egg white, or substitute
with chickpea (garbanzos) water
(aquafaba) to make it vegan

ice cubes, for shaking

lemon peel, to garnish

Combine the ingredients
in a cocktail shaker, top with
ice and shake vigorously for
10 seconds.

Strain into coupe glass and
garnish with a lemon peel.

Raspberry Shrub Sour

You can probably tell I like a sour from the last few recipes.
Pickle juice and shrubs work really well in a sour because
of the sharpness from the vinegar.

Mango

Really refreshing cocktail but with a lot of alcohol! So make sure you have lots of ice whether you're making a jug amongst friends or one, just for yourself. To make this Margarita with the chilli lime salt rim, check out the Michelada (see page 75).

50 ml (2 fl oz) tequila

35 ml (1¼ fl oz) Mango & Ginger
Shrub (see Note)

Serves 1

25 ml (¾ fl oz) orange liqueur

juice of ½ lime (approx.
25 ml/¾ fl oz lime juice)

ice cubes, to serve

Chilli Lime Salt, for rimming
(see page 75)

ice cubes, for shaking

lime slice, to garnish

Note

Make the shrub using
the traditional shrub
method on page 47,
using 2 cups of diced
mango and ½ cup of
grated ginger.

Add a dash of Tobasco
for an extra kick.

You can easily scale-up
the quantities of the
cocktail and serve it in
a pitcher, as shown.

Combine all the ingredients in a
cocktail shaker, top with ice and
shake vigorously for 10 seconds.

Strain over ice into a rocks glass
rimmed with chilli lime salt.
Garnish with a lime slice.

Serves 4

100 ml (3½ fl oz) Raspberry, Strawberry & Blackberry Shrub (see Note)

750 ml (25½ fl oz/3 cups) light dry rosé

150 ml (5 fl oz) soda water (club soda)

agave nectar, for sweetening (optional)

ice cubes, to serve

mint sprig, to garnish

In a large serving jug, build the ingredients over ice, starting with the shrub followed by the rosé and topped up with soda water.

Garnish with a few sprigs of mint, adding more shrub if you'd like it a bit sweeter.

Note

To make the shrub, use the heated shrub method on page 51. I use mixed frozen berries for this too.

If you don't have mint you can also use rosemary or dill.

Summer Berry Shrub Sharer

This cocktail is perfect for sharing with friends. Fill a jug with ice and add a bit of agave nectar if you prefer it a little sweeter. You'll need a big jug for this one as you'll be using a whole bottle of rosé. If you don't have one, try using a big bowl and making it more of a punch styled cocktail.

25 ml (¾ fl oz) Blackberry
& Fresh Thyme Shrub
(see Note)

40 ml (1¼ fl oz) gin

10 ml (¼ fl oz) lemon juice

ice cubes, for shaking

crushed ice, to serve

thyme sprig and blackberries,
to garnish

Combine all the ingredients
in a cocktail shaker, top
with ice cubes and shake
vigorously for 10 seconds.

Strain into a rocks glass over
crushed ice and garnish with
a sprig of lemon thyme.

Serves 1

Bramble

Another one for the gin lovers among us
and makes for a perfect festive cockail.

Note

To make the shrub, use
the heated shrub metho
on page 56, but adding
½ cup of fresh thyme.

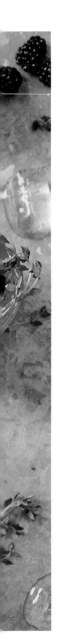

5 ml (⅛ fl oz) Sugar Syrup
(see page 52)

3 dashes Tabasco

25 ml (¾ fl oz) Pickle Juice
(see page 34)

15 ml (½ fl oz) white grappa

50 ml (2 fl oz) dry gin

ice cubes, for shaking

pinch of fresh dill fronds,
to garnish

Serves 1

Muddle all the ingredients
in a cocktail shaker, top with
ice then shake vigorously for
10 seconds.

Strain into a coupe glass and
garnish with a pinch of fresh
dill fronds.

Little Pickle

Named after my little sister, the dill creates a
really nice dill-pickle flavour. See photo overleaf.

Cucumber Shrub Martini

The cucumber shrub adds a nice sweetness to this martini, which is best served really cold.

30 ml (1 fl oz) Cucumber Shrub (see page 48)

50 ml (2 fl oz) Hendrick's gin

15 ml (½ fl oz) Martini bianco vermouth

ice cubes, for shaking

cucumber ribbon, to garnish

Combine the ingredients in a cocktail shaker with the ice and shake vigorously for 10 seconds.

Strain into martini glass and garnish with a cucumber ribbon.

All serve 1

Apple Shrub Soda

This is a super quick, great tasting cocktail. You can easily swap the apple shrub for another shrub you may already have in the fridge.

25 ml (¾ fl oz) Apple Shrub (see Note)

50 ml (2 fl oz) vodka

100 ml (3½ fl oz) soda water (club soda)

ice cubes, to serve

apple slice, (very finely sliced), to garnish

Build all the ingredients over ice in a rocks glass, starting with the apple shrub, then followed by the vodka and soda water. Stir thoroughly.

Garnish with an apple slice.

Note

To make the shrub use the tradtional shrub method on page 47.

Watermelon Mojito

Another great refreshing cocktail for the summer. You can easily double-up the quantities and serve this in a large jug filled with ice.

Muddle the ingredients, except for the crushed ice and watermelon wedges, in a cocktail shaker then build in a highball glass over crushed ice. You don't need to strain this as you want to incorporate all the muddled mint leaves and flavours.

Garnish with a few wedges of watermelon and a sprig of mint.

40 ml (1¼ fl oz) dark rum

50 ml (2 fl oz) Watermelon Shrub (see page 53)

1 teaspoon lime juice

1 teaspoon brown sugar

10 fresh mint leaves

crushed ice, to serve

watermelon wedges and a mint sprig, to garnish

From left to right: Cucumber Shrub Martini, Apple Shrub Soda and Watermelon Mojito

Chasers

If you've got a bottle of pickle juice ready to go in the fridge, these chasers are great for when you have a group of friends over. Drink the shot of spirit, followed by the shot of pickle juice or shrub. The sharp shot of alcohol 'chased' by the punchy pickle juice really balances out the flavours, while also mellowing out the alcoholic 'burn' you sometimes get. Now these are true love-it-or-hate-it kinds of drinks, and they're bound to divide opinion in the room, but that's what makes it fun!

**All chasers
serve 1**

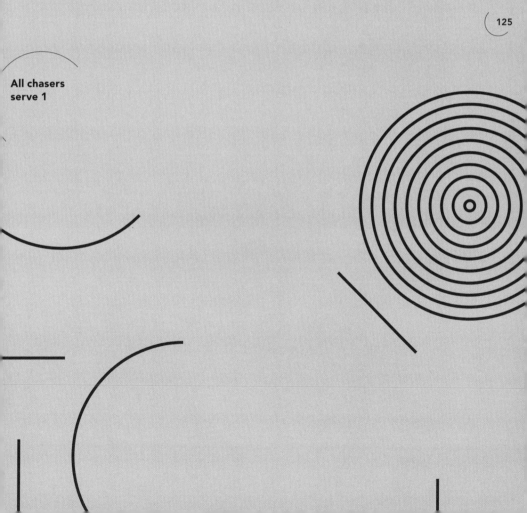

126

Holy Maria

Hot Smoked Chilliback

Pickleback

Holy Maria

25 ml (¾ fl oz) tequila

25 ml (¾ fl oz) Original Bloody Mary,
without the vodka (with a squeeze of lime)
(see page 72)

—

Using two shot glasses, shot the tequila
followed by the Bloody Mary.

Hot Smoked Chilliback

25 ml (¾ fl oz) Mezcal

25 ml (¾ fl oz) Spicy Dill Pickle Juice
(see page 35)

—

Using two shot glasses, shot the Mezcal
followed by the dill pickle juice.

Pickleback

25 ml (¾ fl oz) whisky (I like to use bourbon)

25 ml (¾ fl oz) Pickle Juice
(see page 34)

—

Using two shot glasses, shot the whisky
followed by the pickle juice.

What a Melon

25 ml (¾ fl oz) gin

25 ml (¾ fl oz) Watermelon Shrub
(see page 53)

—

Using two shot glasses, shot the gin
followed by the watermelon shrub.

So you Soju

25 ml (¾ fl oz) Soju

25 ml (¾ fl oz) Kimchi Juice
(see page 38)

—

Using two shot glasses, shot the Soju
followed by the kimchi pickle juice.

Sweet & Sour Pickleback

25 ml (¾ fl oz) whisky

25 ml (¾ fl oz) Sweet Vietnamese Vinegar
(see page 45)

—

Using two shot glasses, shot the whisky
followed by the sweet Vietnamese vinegar.

What a Melon

So You Soju

Sweet & Sour Pickleback

Non-
alcoholic

Cocktails

Shrubs are a great alternative to alcoholic cocktails; the acidity from the vinegar adds a similar depth of flavour as spirits. My preference is to use one part shrub to three parts soda water (club soda), but mix it according to your taste. With all the drinks in this section, I have suggested the perfect alcohol to pair with it, because, well, it's good to have the option! They taste great either way, so the choice is yours.

Beetroot & Apple Shrub Soda

This is my favourite shrub soda. Beetroot on its own works really well too and has an amazing colour.

50 ml (2 fl oz) Beetroot & Apple Shrub (see page 52)

150 ml (5 fl oz) soda water (club soda)

ice cubes, to serve

apple slice, to garnish

Build the ingredients over ice in a rocks glass, starting with the shrub, then topped with soda water.

Garnish with an apple slice.

Make it alcoholic

Add a shot (50 ml/2 fl oz) of gin or vodka.

Both serve 1

Spinach, Cucumber & Mint Shrub Soda

Make this shrub soda by using the quick shrub method on page 51.

soda water (club soda), to serve

ice cubes, to serve

cucumber slice, to garnish

Shrub

1 cucumber, cut into cubes

100 g (3½ oz/2 cups) spinach

4 mint sprigs

50 ml (2 fl oz) Sugar Syrup (see page 52)

50 ml (2 fl oz) apple cider vinegar

Using the quick shrub method, juice the cucumber, spinach and mint together. Pour into a bowl and add the sugar syrup and vinegar. Stir thoroughly.

Build all the ingredients in a rocks glass over ice, starting with the shrub, then top with soda water.

Garnish with a cucumber slice.

Make it alcoholic

Add a shot (25 ml/¾ fl oz) of gin.

25 ml (¾ fl oz) Carrot Pickle Juice (see page 44)

15 ml (½ fl oz) Ginger & Demerara Sugar Shrub (see page 98)

50 ml (2 fl oz) good-quality lemonade

soda water (club soda)

ice cubes, to serve

squeeze of lime juice

lime slice, to garnish

Build the ingredients in a highball glass filled with ice, starting with the carrot pickle juice, then the shrub, then the lemonade. Give it a stir, taste then top with soda water and a squeeze of lime juice.

Garnish with a lime slice.

Make it alcoholic

Add a shot (50 ml/2 fl oz) of tequila

Carrot & Ginger Shrub Soda

Try this carrot and ginger health tonic with a good-quality lemonade, as it makes a real difference.

25 ml (¾ fl oz) Ginger &
Demerara Sugar Shrub
(see Note on page 98)

50 ml (2 fl oz) grapefruit juice

ice cubes, for shaking

soda water (club soda), to serve

ice cubes, to serve

slice of grapefruit and sprig of
rosemary, to garnish

Combine the shrub and
grapefruit juice in a cocktail
shaker with the ice and shake
vigorously for 10 seconds.

Strain into a coupe glass
filled with ice, and top with
soda water. Garnish with the
rosemary sprig.

Make it alcoholic

Add a shot (50 ml/2 fl oz)
of silver tequila.

Ginger & Demerara Paloma

Using Demerara sugar in a shrub adds a really nice richness
to the flavour. Combine with grapefruit juice, it makes for a
great Paloma.

25 ml (¾ fl oz) Strawberry
& Basil Shrub (see Note)

50 ml (2 fl oz) lime juice
(approx. 1 lime)

50 ml (2 fl oz) good-quality
apple juice

25 ml (¾ fl oz) soda water
(club soda)

ice cubes, for shaking

crushed ice, to serve

macerated strawberries,
to garnish

Note

To make the shrub use the
traditional shrub method
on page 47, but add ½ cup
of basil leaves.

Combine all the ingredients in
a cocktail shaker, top with ice
cubes and shake vigorously for
10 seconds.

Strain into rocks glass over
crushed ice and garnish with
a few macerated strawberries.

Make it alcoholic

Add a shot (50 ml/2 fl oz) of
white rum.

Strawberry Crush

This is a great non-alcoholic take on the strawberry daiquiri
and can be doubled up as a dessert. You could even try
adding whipped cream or a scoop of ice cream topped with
macerated strawberries to make it even more indulgent.

50 ml (2 fl oz) Seedlip Garden

25 ml (¾ fl oz) Cucumber & Elderflower Shrub (see Note)

100 ml (3½ fl oz) tonic water

ice cubes, to serve

cucumber ribbon, to garnish

Build the cocktail in a rocks glass filled with ice, starting with the Seedlip, then the shrub and finishing with the tonic water.

Garnish with a thin ribbon of cucumber and enjoy.

Make it alcoholic

Swap the Seedlip for gin.

Note

Use the traditional shrub method on page 47, adding 1 cup of elderflower cordial.

Seedlip Garden

with a Cucumber & Elderflower Shrub Tonic

If you haven't heard of Seedlip, now's the time. It's the first non-alcoholic spirit of its kind, and it's a perfect alternative if you're skipping the booze.

Serves 1

50 ml (2 fl oz) Cinnamon &
Apple Shrub (see page 61)

15 ml (½ fl oz) Honey or agave
nectar

15 ml (½ fl oz) lemon juice

boiling water, to serve

cinnamon stick and slice of
lemon, to garnish

Build all the ingredients in a
rocks glass, starting with the
cinnamon and apple shrub,
then the honey or agave
nectar and then the lemon
juice. Top with boiling water.

Garnish with a cinnamon stick
and slice of lemon.

Make it alcoholic

Add a shot (25 ml/¾ fl oz)
of whisky.

Apple and Cinnamon Shrub Toddy

The perfect winter warmer for those cold nights in.
It's also a great sore throat soother. If you'd like to make
more than one serving, try doubling the quantities (or more)
and add all the ingredients into a saucepan, bringing the
water to the boil. Then ladle out into mugs or glasses.

50 ml (2 fl oz) Kimchi Juice
(see page 39)

75 ml (2½ fl oz) beetroot juice

1 teaspoon Sriracha

1 teaspoon sesame oil

pinch of coarsely ground black
pepper

ice cubes, to serve

kimchi, to garnish

Serves 1

Build the ingredients over ice in
a highball glass starting with the
kimchi juice, then the beetroot
juice, followed by the Sriracha,
sesame oil and black pepper.

Garnish with a piece of kimchi.

Make it alcoholic

Add a shot (25 ml/¾ fl oz)
of vodka.

Kimchi Spiced Beet

A variation of the Kimchi Bloody Mary (see page 78),
this one uses beetroot juice to add an earthy flavour.

Bo

Recommended

East London Liquor Company Vodka, Gin, Rum and Whisky

These guys are great, the first vodka, gin, rum and whisky distillery in East London. Alex Wolpert, the founder, used to work at one of the first pubs in East London that I sold a bottle of pickle juice to.

Flint and Hardings Vodka and Gin

My Mum has recently started making a vodka and gin using the sugar beetroot from my grandparent's farm. I know I'm biased, but it's absolutely delicious and because it's made with sugar beetroots it's completely gluten free, unlike many vodkas and gins.

Sipsmith Vodka and Gin

Love Sipsmith! To me they're the ones that were really at the forefront of the gin revolution.

They also make a great vodka. Last summer they hosted an amazing Bloody Mary ambulance using our spiced tomato mix and going around the campsites at festivals in a golf buggy serving hungover campers Bloody Marys.

Our/London Vodka

Our/London is based in Hackney but they also have many other 'Our/ vodkas' across the world. I love using their vodka in my Bloody Marys. We've done many events with them and they hosted the launch of our Bloody Mary mix at their distillery, which is definitely worth a visit.

Chase Vodka and Gin

These guys represent all things truly British and have gone from potato farmers to crisp makers all the way through to vodka and gin makers!

Absolut Vodka

Always a good go-to premium quality vodka that is found in most retailers. Owned by Pernod Ricard, they're a great company who we collaborated with a lot in our early pickle juice days.

Jameson Whisky

Thought I'd go on to Jameson next as they're also from the Pernod Ricard family. Their whisky is great for Picklebacks.

Nikka Whisky

My favourite! This Japanese whisky is really smooth and a great addition to cocktails and a great for a Pickleback.

Jensen's Gin

Small batch gin distillery in Bermondsey using all the traditional gin botanicals. It makes for a really flavourful Red Snapper.

Dodd's Gin

I first tried this gin because I was drawn to its label. It is made with organic botanicals, including honey from The London Honey Company.

Olmeca Altos Tequila

Award-winning Mexican tequila using 100% Agave Tequila, super smooth, great on its own or in a Margarita.

Seedlip Garden

For those not drinking, Seedlip is the world's first non-alcoholic spirit available in two flavours: Garden 108 and Spice 94. A great alternative to gin, try our Seedlip Garden with Cucumber & Elderflower Shrub Tonic recipe (see page 143).

Florence Cherruault is the founder of the award-winning drinks company, The Pickle House.

Producing a pickle juice and Bloody Mary mix, which are stocked in bars, restaurants, hotels and selected retailers across the UK. Having always been a huge fan of all things pickled, she was one of the first people to start making pickle juice specifically for the drinks industry in London after falling in love with drinking it in New York.

About the Author

An absolutely huge thank you to everyone who helped put this book together, especially the team at Hardie Grant and Kajal Mistry, who asked if I could write a book about pickle juice. Kajal, you've been incredible at helping me translate everything in my head to a book, I think it's also helped a lot that we've both had the same vision for what it should look like.

Thanks also to the whole gang at the photoshoot, you guys were unbelievable. Clare Lewington you've made this book come alive with your beautiful photography, seriously great work, thank you. Holly Cowgill your styling went beyond anything I could have imagined, you came up with some really great set-ups and I won't forget your great hands. Gwill Wales, cocktail maker extraordinaire and Emma Guscott for being a fabulous photographer's assistant. Ginger Whisk for their amazing props and range of glassware. Huge thanks to Matt Russell and Simon Sorted at The Grocery Studios for having us and letting us stink up your studio with pickles for a week.

Thank you to Andrea O'Connor for your feedback and great edits on the book.

Trev and Mike from NotOnSunday, LOVE the designs, layout and front cover, you guys smashed it!

Thanks to my main man Tim Jackson, I couldn't do it without you. To my amazing family, my mum who's been by my side since the very first bottle of pickle juice, my sisters Chessy and Noodle, my dad, Paul and Claire.

Big thanks to Portia Butterworth for making sure all my words made sense during the first edits, Ned Stone for keeping The Pickle House going whilst I was writing and Vicky Dalton-Banks for helping test out the recipes.

Thank you

Index

Published in 2019 by Hardie Grant Books, an imprint of Hardie Grant Publishing

Hardie Grant Books (London)
5th & 6th Floors
52–54 Southwark Street
London SE1 1UN

Hardie Grant Books (Melbourne)
Building 1, 658 Church Street
Richmond, Victoria 3121

hardiegrantbooks.com

British Library Cataloguing-in-Publication Data. A catalogue record for this book is available from the British Library.

Pickle Juice by Florence Cherruault
ISBN: 978-1-78488-189-4

Publisher: Kate Pollard
Commissioning Editor: Kajal Mistry
Art Direction and Illustrations: NotOnSunday
Recipe Editor: Andrea O'Connor
Photographer: Clare Lewington
Photography Assistant: Emma Guscott
Author photo on page 153 © Issy Croker
Food Stylist and Hand Model: Holly Cowgill
Cocktail Maker: Gwill Wales
Prop Stylist: Ginger Whisk
Indexer: Cathy Heath

Colour Reproduction by p2d
Printed and bound in China by Leo Paper Group